What's it like to be a...

FISHERMAN

Written by Janet Craig
Illustrated by Allan Eitzen

Troll Associates

Special Consultant: Captain James Coronesi, *Cor-J Fishing Station, Hampton Bays, New York.*

Library of Congress Cataloging-in-Publication Data

Craig, Janet.
    Fisherman / by Janet Craig; illustrated by Allan
Eitzen.
      p.   cm.—(What's it like to be a...)
    Summary: Follows the daily activities of a fisherman as he and his
partner take their boat out on the ocean, bring back a big catch of
fish, and sell the fish at the market.
    ISBN 0-8167-1438-X (lib. bdg.)   ISBN 0-8167-1439-8 (pbk.)
    1. Fishers—Juvenile literature. [1. Fishers. 2. Occupations.]
I. Eitzen, Allan, ill. II. Title. III. Series.
HD8039.F65P35 1989
639.2′023′73—dc19   88-10045

What's it like to be a...
FISHERMAN

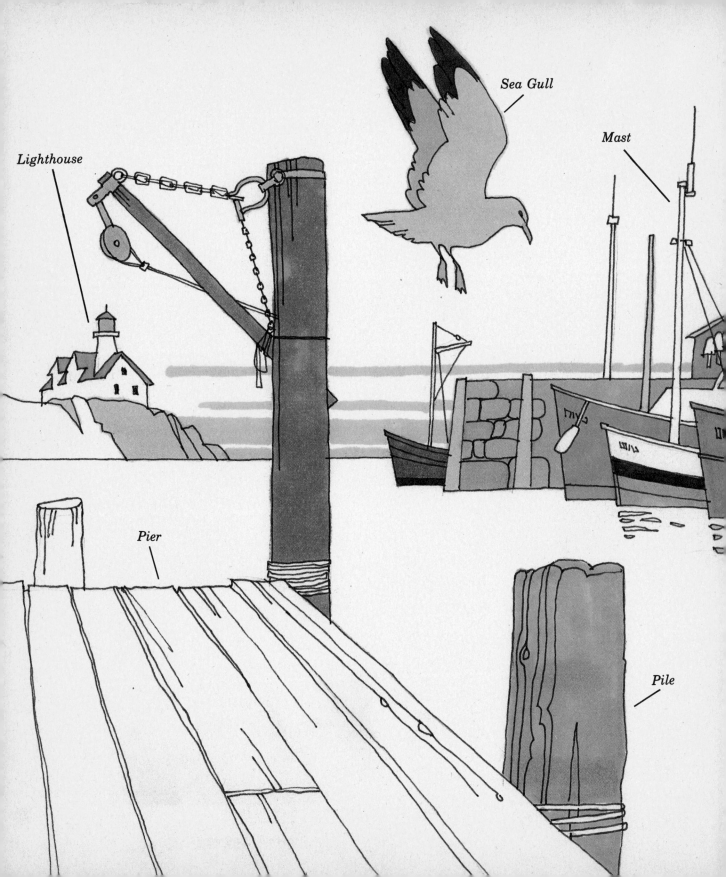

Lighthouse

Sea Gull

Mast

Pier

Pile

Shroud

82077010

780325

A gentle summer breeze blows. It's early
morning at the fishing pier. A sea gull flies high
above the many boats tied to the dock. Then it
lands on a rough post and looks about.

Here comes Andy. He's a fisherman. He's up early and on his way to meet his brother Dan. Today they plan to take their boat out on the ocean and bring back a big catch of fish. Then they will sell the fish at market.

Pile

Waterproof Coveralls

"Hi, Dan," calls Andy. "Ready to cast off?"
"As soon as you take a look at those fishing
lines," answers Dan.

Andy jumps aboard. Their sturdy, small fishing boat is named the *Porpoise*. It's been to sea many times. On its crowded deck are tubs full of long lines.

Andy checks the lines. Dan makes sure there is enough fuel for the trip. He also checks to see if the boat's radio is working. In case of trouble or bad weather, the brothers will use the radio to signal for help.

Grab Rails

Tubs

Hooks & Lines

Gunwale

Cleat

Hatch Cover

Deep Well Vent

Radio Antenna

Loran Navigator

Deep Well

Engine Gauges

Wheel

Sonar
(Finding Fish)

Throttle

Radio

Forward/Reverse Lever

"All ready here," calls Andy. "Let's go!"

Dan starts the engine. Andy loosens the ropes that hold the boat to the dock.

Away chugs the *Porpoise,* ready for a day of work. The sun glitters on the water. Dan looks back at the pier. It looks smaller and smaller as the boat travels further from shore.

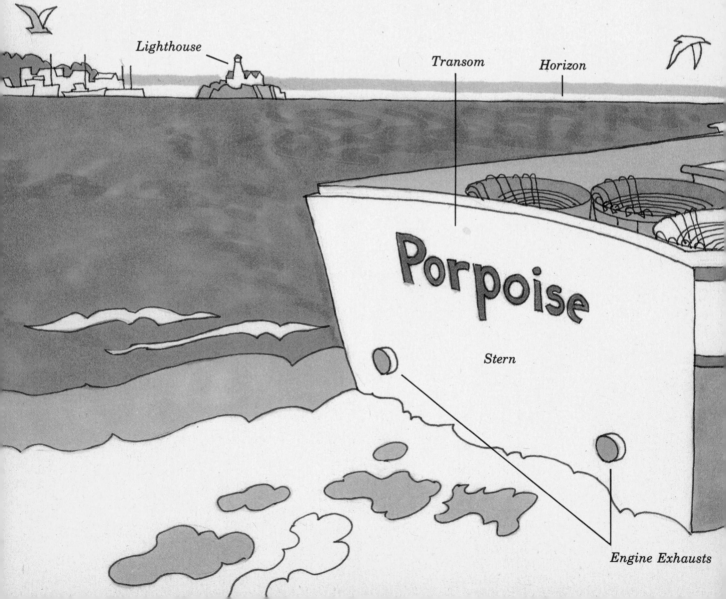

Lighthouse

Transom

Horizon

Porpoise

Stern

Engine Exhausts

Wheel House

Bow

Wake

11

Far away, Andy spots several small boats. They are near a rocky part of the shore. The men aboard are busy lowering special traps into the icy water.

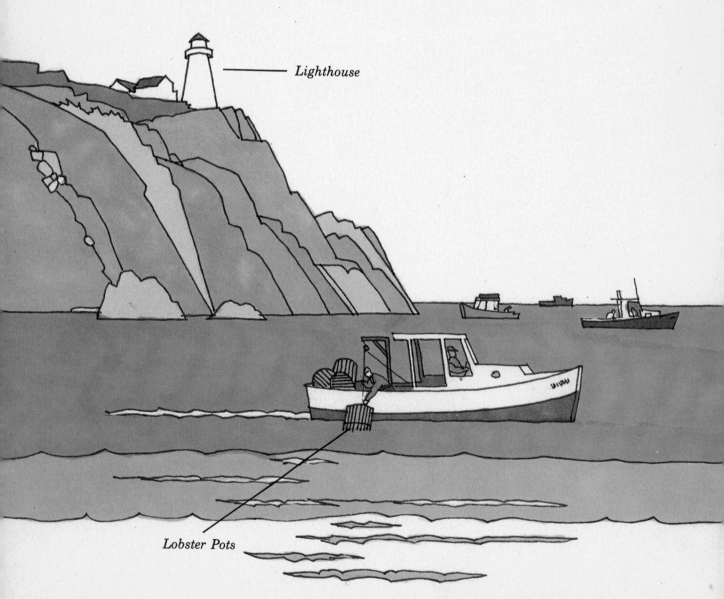

Lighthouse

Lobster Pots

These men hope to catch many of the strange-looking animals called lobsters. The tasty lobster can be sold at the fish market for a very high price.

Lobster Pots

KAT

Lobstermen know where the best feeding
grounds of the lobster are. Every morning, the
men lower their wooden traps, called lobster pots,
into the water. Inside each trap is a bit of fish or
other bait. The lobster can easily get into the
trap to eat the bait. But a net inside the trap
makes it hard for the lobster to get out.

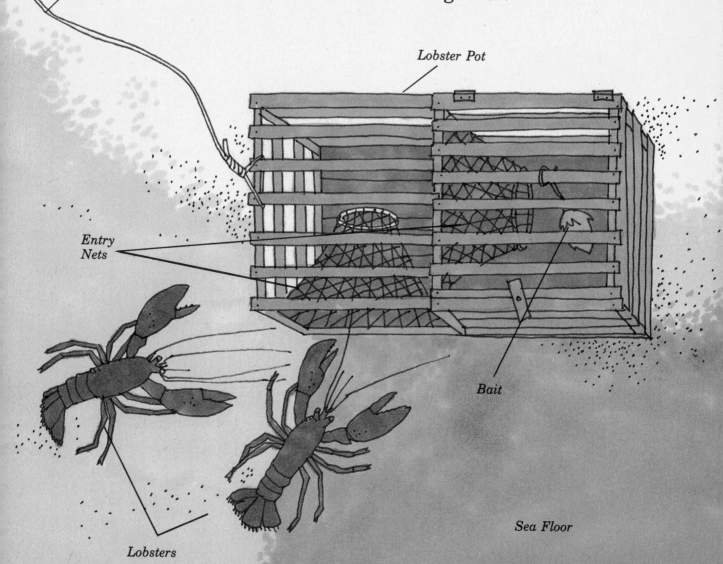

Buoy Line

Lobster Pot

Entry
Nets

Bait

Lobsters

Sea Floor

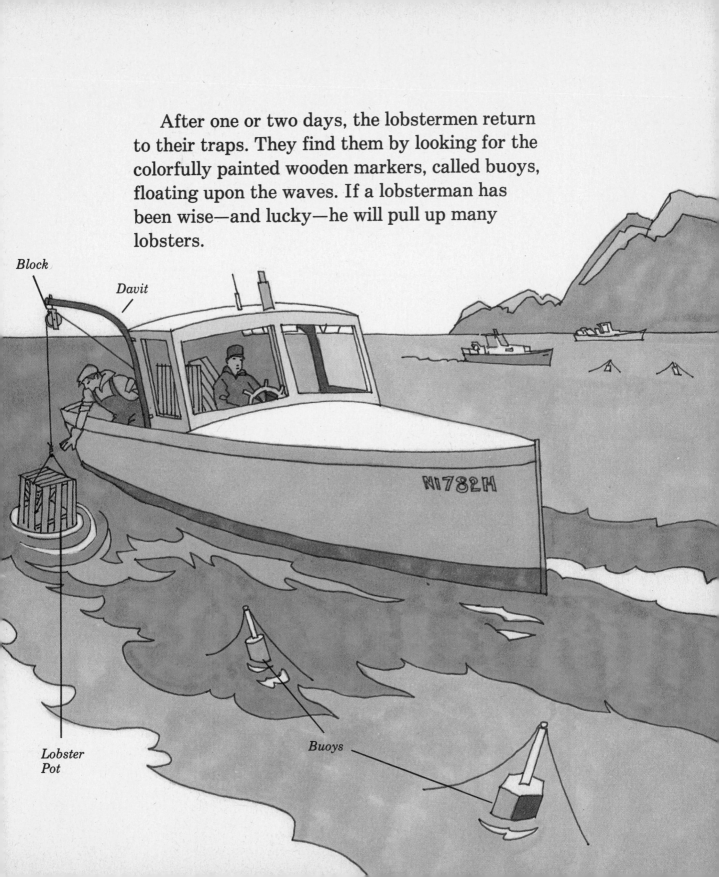

After one or two days, the lobstermen return to their traps. They find them by looking for the colorfully painted wooden markers, called buoys, floating upon the waves. If a lobsterman has been wise—and lucky—he will pull up many lobsters.

Block

Davit

Lobster Pot

Buoys

N1782H

Good fishermen always know the habits and
feeding grounds of the fish they want to catch.
"Are we there yet?" Andy calls to Dan.
"Soon," answers Dan.

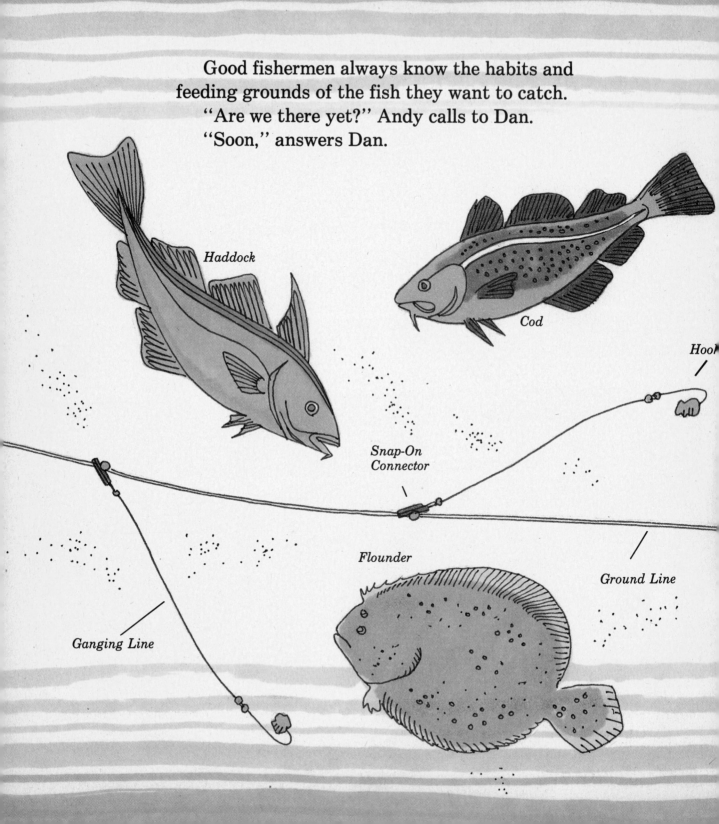

Haddock

Cod

Hook

Snap-On
Connector

Ground Line

Flounder

Ganging Line

Dan and Andy are looking for haddock, a kind
of fish that finds its food upon the ocean floor.
The two brothers are good at catching haddock.
But often they are surprised at the many
different kinds of fish they pull in. Pollock,
flounder, cod, halibut—even sharks—have been
caught.

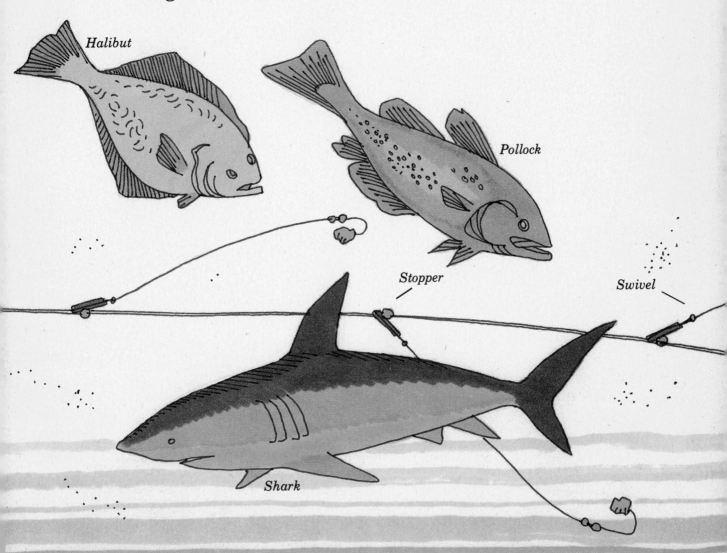

Halibut

Pollock

Stopper

Swivel

Shark

Dan checks their course. He sees that they
have reached the spot they are looking for. This
is a place where haddock often come to feed.
"Get the lines ready," Dan calls.

Wet (Liquid) Compass

Engine Gauges

Andy and Dan are a special kind of fishermen.
They are called trawl, or long line, fishermen.
They catch fish by lowering very long lines into
the water. Connected to the long lines are many
shorter lines filled with baited hooks.

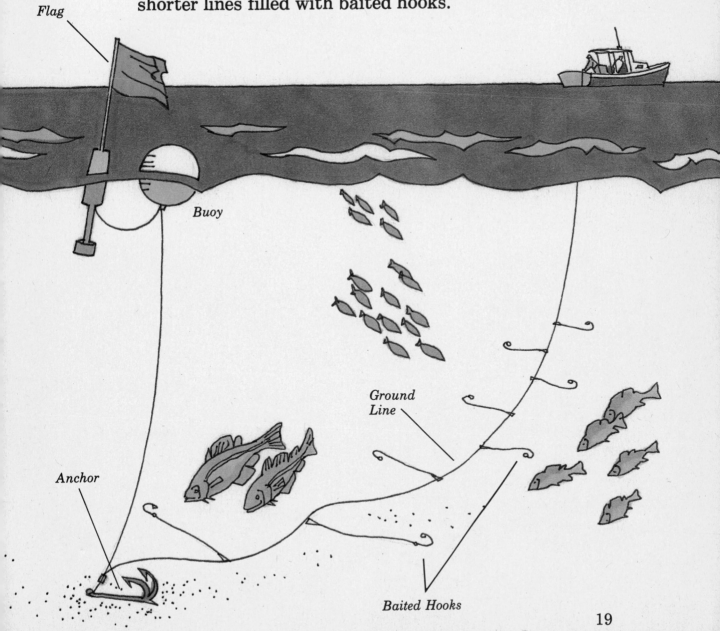

Flag

Buoy

*Ground
Line*

Anchor

Baited Hooks

19

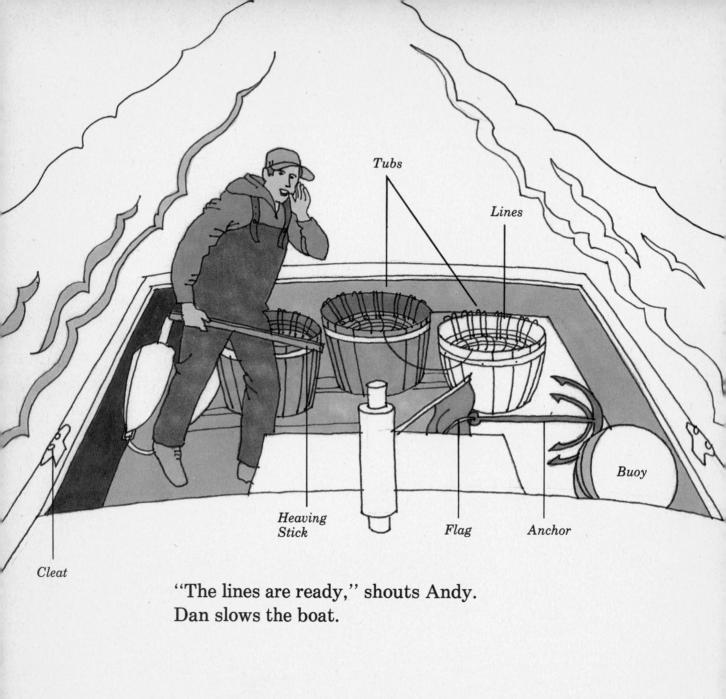

Tubs

Lines

Heaving
Stick

Flag

Anchor

Buoy

Cleat

"The lines are ready," shouts Andy.
Dan slows the boat.

Andy puts on heavy gloves. He heaves an anchor, a flag, and a buoy into the water. Then, from the big tubs, Andy begins to throw out the long line. He uses a special stick to lift out the coils of line. The hooks are sharp! Andy is careful not to get too close to them.

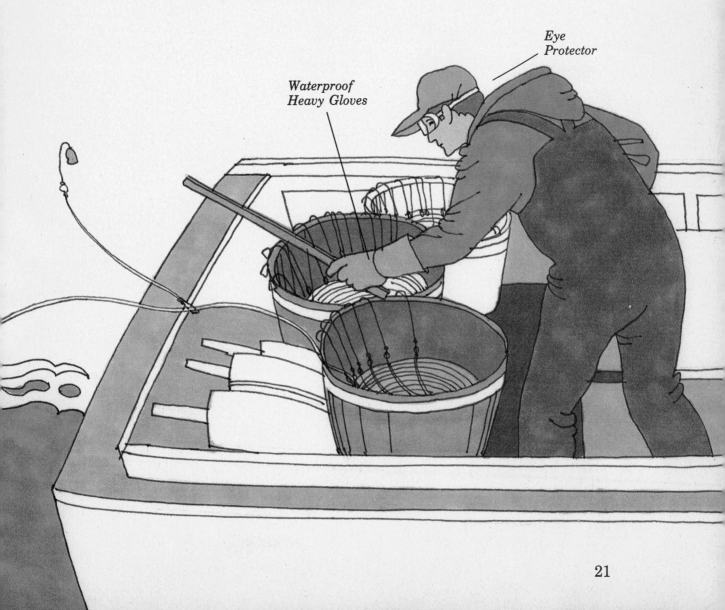

Eye
Protector

Waterproof
Heavy Gloves

The brothers work very hard. At last, the first line has been set out. Andy and Dan exchange places. Andy steers the *Porpoise*. And now it is Dan's turn to set out the second long line.

With two lines set, the brothers take a short break for lunch. Then it's back to work. The brothers find their way back to the flag, which marks the place where the first line was set.

Andy pulls up the line a bit. Then he smiles a big smile. The line is full of haddock.

"We're in luck today!" he calls.

Deep Well

The heavy work of hauling in the catch
begins. The brothers lift the glistening fish into
the boat. Then the fish are dumped into a cold
compartment to keep them fresh.

Gaff

"Look at this one," calls Dan.

Andy looks and sees a huge halibut on one of the lines. It will bring a good price. To lift the heavy fish, Dan uses a gaff, a strong pole with a hook at the end.

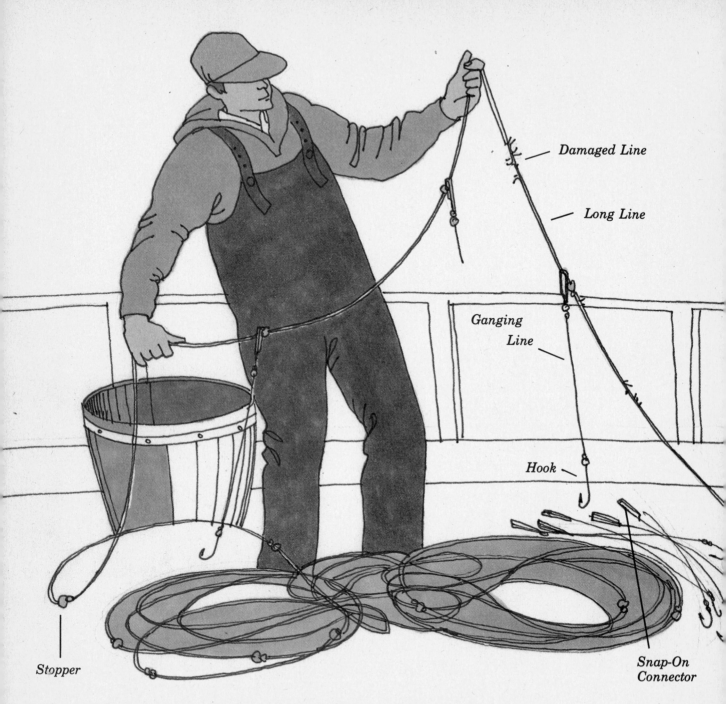

Damaged Line

Long Line

Ganging Line

Hook

Stopper

Snap-On Connector

After all the fish have been taken aboard,
Andy looks over the lines. They are still in good
shape—only a few need to be fixed.

The brothers start for home. But their work is
not done yet. During the trip back, they must
prepare the fish.

Tubs

Knife

Heavy Gloves

A cloud of shrieking sea gulls follows the *Porpoise*. The hungry birds hope to catch a bit of fish that may be thrown overboard.

At last, the brothers dock their boat. Now they must unload their catch. The pier is bustling. A big fishing boat has just pulled into dock. Workers hurry back and forth. Gulls are crying out. Long trucks are driving into place.

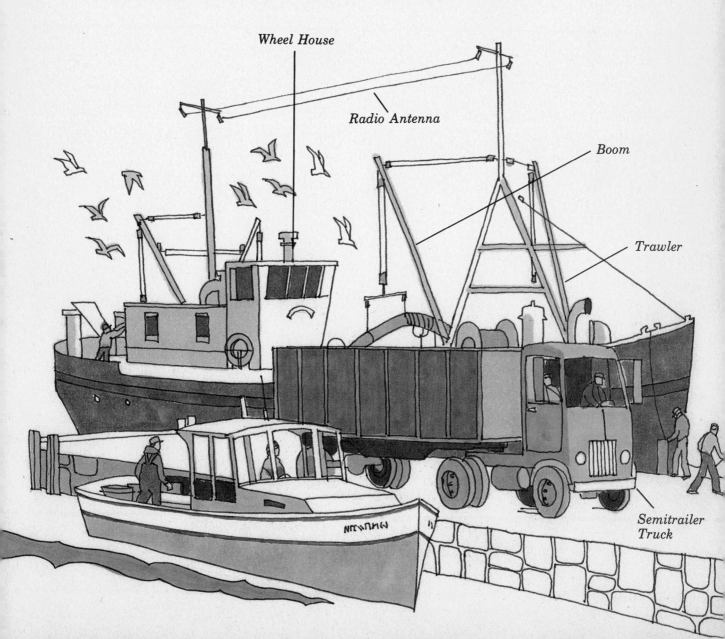

Wheel House

Radio Antenna

Boom

Trawler

Semitrailer Truck

This large boat is called a trawler. Much bigger than the *Porpoise,* the trawler is made for catching codfish. It goes far out to sea for weeks at a time and carries a big crew.

Instead of using lines, the trawler drags a huge cone-shaped net, called an otter trawl, along the ocean floor. This net can catch as much as five thousand pounds of fish in one hour.

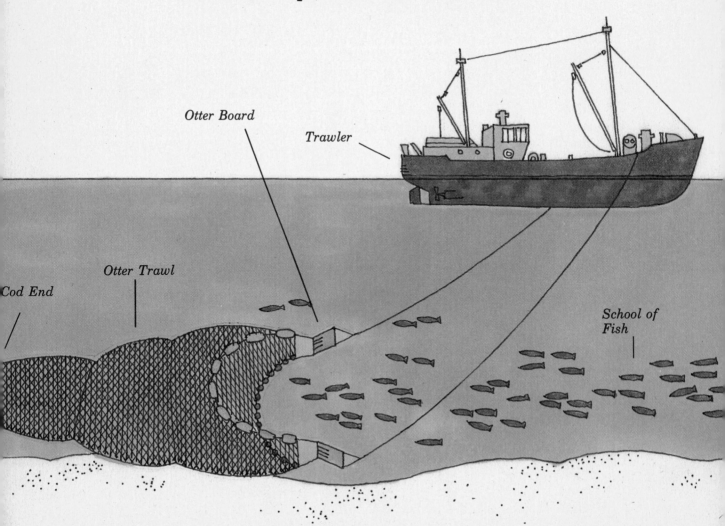

Otter Board

Trawler

Otter Trawl

Cod End

School of Fish

Chute

There's much excitement as this trawler unloads its catch. Machinery *whirs* and grinds. Thousands of slippery gray cod pour down chutes into the waiting trucks. The fish will be rushed to factories to be cleaned and frozen.

Andy has always loved to watch the activity at the fishing pier. He stops to look at the big trawler—but only for a moment. He and Dan must finish putting the catch into their truck. Then, with a big wave, Dan drives away to the fish market.

Now the sun is setting. Andy looks out over the calm ocean. It's been a good catch and a busy day. With a smile—and a big yawn—Andy heads for home.